Friends to Keep in Art and Life

Friends

to Keep

in Art

and Life

Nicole Tersigni
Foreword by Sara Benincasa

CHRONICLE BOOKS

Library of Congress Cataloging-in-Publication Data

Names: Tersigni, Nicole, author.
Title: Friends to keep in art and life / Nicole Tersigni ; foreword by Sara Benincasa.
Description: San Francisco : Chronicle Books, 2022. | Includes
bibliographical references.
Identifiers: LCCN 2021049598 | ISBN 9781797216300 (hardback)
Subjects: LCSH: Female friendship. | Friendship--Pictorial works. |
Interpersonal relations. | Art--Humor.
Classification: LCC BF575.F66 T48 2022 | DDC 302.34082--dc23/eng/20211216
LC record available at https://lccn.loc.gov/2021049598

ISBN 978-1-7972-1630-0

Manufactured in China.

Designed by Maggie Edelman.

10 9 8 7 6 5 4 3 2 1

Chronicle Books LLC
680 Second Street
San Francisco, CA 94107
www.chroniclebooks.com

For gal pals everywhere,
but especially mine.

In the words of Galentine's Day
founder, Leslie Knope, you're
all poetic, noble land-mermaids.

Foreword

There is nothing in the world as wonderful as a good friend. Sure, orgasms are great (and friends can help you have them), but they don't last particularly long. Bread is fantastic, but if it's in my house, it does not last very long, either. Unlike orgasms and bread, friendships can last a lifetime.

In *Friends to Keep in Art and Life*, the delightful follow-up to her marvelous *Men to Avoid in Art and Life*, Nicole Tersigni has cleverly categorized friendships: the Work Friend, the Nurturing Friend, the Hide a Body for You Friend, the Up for Anything Friend, and the Super Honest Friend. Where do your best friends fit? You should probably tell them in the loving inscription you write when you gift this book to them!

I am so grateful to be blessed with friends in every category, even some who encompass multiple categories. I must especially celebrate Gretchen, my friend since fifth grade, and Katherine, my friend since college (the one that I would eventually drop out of). They are wonderful humans, community members, mothers, wives, adult children to their parents, and fantastic friends to me and various others.

But not all friendships need to be so established. As you'll see in this book, it can be just as much of a joy to have a Work Friend with whom you talk shit about the lesser beings in your professional midst. The Up for Anything Friend is the spontaneous, party-loving pal you need to get you out of a funk. The Super Honest Friend, no matter how harsh, only has the best intentions when they tell you exactly what you need to hear exactly when you need to hear it. The Nurturing Friend always has extra supplies for whatever fluids may escape any orifice at any time. The Hide a Body for You Friend is your ride-or-die BFF, or perhaps just somebody loyal who enjoys criminal subterfuge.

Either way, count yourself lucky to have acquired Nicole's latest book. It is fucking hilarious. And you might learn something about art, too! While lately I've been spending time with the more contemporary works of Bisa Butler, Kehinde Wiley, and Maya Erdelyi-Perez, I have greatly enjoyed Nicole's vivid commentary paired with the art of talented dead guys such as Henri de Toulouse-Lautrec, Edgar Degas, and Ulrich Apt the Elder. Imagine saying that last one out loud during sex. What a dream!

May you and your friends enjoy this book, and spend lots of time taking snapshots of the pages and sending them to one another saying, "This is definitely us."

Love,
Sara Benincasa

The Work Friend

"... and then he explained to me
what a pivot table is."
"But you're the head of analytics."
"I'm the fucking head of analytics."

"I can't believe they promoted Diane over us.

She doesn't know her asshole from a purl stitch."

"Her asshole is the thing on her

face that never stops moving."

"Good one."

12

"These new healthy snacks from corporate smell like tree farts."

"Taste like them, too. Wanna split my emergency cheese sandwich?"

13

"Do you think anyone will know
we had drinks at lunch?"
"Our tits are out. So…they might."

"I wish we could just quit…"

"Let's do it. Earlier I clicked a link for 'You Won't Believe Which Celebrity Has a Secret Second Butt!' but it was a virus, and now I can't get into my computer, so the timing is perfect."

"It might be the edible talking, but we're the best employees this company has ever had."

"Totally. How long have we been on break?"

"Only five minutes. Wait, no, five hours. Somewhere between five minutes and five hours."

"I can't believe Todd repeated your idea in the meeting like he came up with it."
"So glad we used his personal microwave."
"Hope you like the smell of reheated salmon, Todd."

"Tell me why we have to dress like Laura Ingalls Wilder, but the men get to walk around in shorts."

"If they saw a woman's bare leg, their boners would explode, I guess."

"Table eight sent their burgers back
again and called me a moron."
"We'll handle this.
I hope they like spit burgers."

"Yes, you accidentally emailed our boss saying you
have stanky swamp ass. Yes, he's very handsome,
and yes, that was embarrassing."
"But?"
"That's all I got."

"Putting turtles in the break room was one of your top three ideas."

"Better or worse than making Brian's screen saver a picture of them humping?"

"... and then he asked if it came in a manlier shade of pink."

"Ugh. Sir, this is a flower shop, not a penis-measuring store."

24

"Did you hear Trent lecture Barb about using social media at work? Meanwhile he was swiping on Tinder during the marketing meeting."

"Careful, he has spies everywhere.
Yes, we see you lurking in the doorway, Dolores."

"I don't want to do team bonding with those weirdos."

"Remember the ropes course?"

"I still think about Pam hanging upside down and screaming about her wedgie."

"And then write, 'It's for these reasons that I believe I deserve a raise.'"

"But maybe take out the part where you call him a condescending cock weasel."

The Nurturing Friend

"Take an Advil, drink a full glass of water, and get some sleep."

"I think I drew a wiener on the bathroom stall."

"You did. Huge balls. Go to bed."

"Did you put on sunblock?"
"Yes. Of course."
"I just don't want your butt
cheeks to burn like last time."
"The peeling stage was embarrassing.
So much scratching."

"...and the princess punched the prince in his stupid cheating face, and her best friend kicked him in the balls. Then they celebrated with bottomless cheese fries."

"Text me a picture of your driver, their license plate, and your date. And tell him your best friend knows his face so he's too nervous to murder you."

"Your doctor said no getting up while you're recovering, so if you try and get out of this bed, I will flatten you. And that can't be good for your stitches."

"As much as I love listening to your drunk asses scream-singing 'Party in the U.S.A.,' we should go. Check each other for ticks, don't make eye contact with that weirdo, and help me gather up your bras."

34

"Spent a hundred dollars on face cream and I still look old."

"Because we are old. That's okay. You know who else is old?
The Sistine fucking Chapel. And that shit's beautiful."

"It's beautiful. Looks like something from the Louvre. You're so talented."

"It's only half an eyeball so far."

"But it's the most beautiful half an eyeball I've ever seen."

"Oh my god, you guys, did I send that selfie to Sam last night?"

"First of all, it was just a close-up of your left boob.
Second, you sent it to your mom.
Third, we took your phone so you couldn't send a photo of the right one too."

"Before we go to this party, what else do I need to put in my purse? I've got snacks, ChapStick, pads, wipes, a pocketknife, pepper spray, Band-Aids, Kleenex, mace, Lactaid, and jumper cables."

"Listen to me. You are the world's best mother."

"I'm so tired."

"I'll watch them while you nap. Which one's the biter?"

"All of them."

39

"You look exhausted. I'm going to draw you a bath with some of my best essential oils. This one is called Essence of Dolly Parton. It's lavender, chamomile, and stardust."

"I'm going to pin your dress up

so you stop tripping on it."

"Why do you bring safety

pins to the club?"

"Why *don't* you?"

"Remember when I was sick and you cleaned up after me?"

"It was the grossest day of my life, but that's what friends are for."

"It was geysering from both ends."

"Yes. I remember."

42

The Hide a Body for You Friend

"He said my pepperoni nipples were too aggressive."

"It's going to be really aggressive when I shit on his porch."

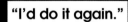

"Your mom said your art was bad, so what? She has a poster of the *Mona Lisa* saying 'Live, Laugh, Love.' What does she know?"

"That woman said my dress is the second ugliest thing she's ever seen, after my hat."

"Say the word, and I will strangle her with my enormous butt bow."

"Those two are talking shit about your dress, so I ordered fifty pizzas on their tab."

"Let me handle this creep. You just got your nails done."

"What did you just say to my best friend? I will drag you into the lake by that muppet-skin merkin you call pubic hair."

"When I die, I'm going to
haunt all of our enemies."
"I love that."
"And spy on hot people
in the shower."
"I bet ghosts spy on
us all the time."

"I love you, and I support you, but if your boyfriend makes one more 'joke' about your cooking, I'm going stab him with your hat pin."

"Are those bitches talking about us?"
"If they are, I'm ready to throw down."
"You guys want to fight everyone."
"Only everyone who tries to fuck with us."

"I listen to enough true crime podcasts that I could commit the perfect murder."

"It was just one bad date, so I don't think we need to go there yet. But good to know."

"If he didn't want me to fill his gas tank with minestrone, he shouldn't have dumped you at an Olive Garden."

The Up for Anything Friend

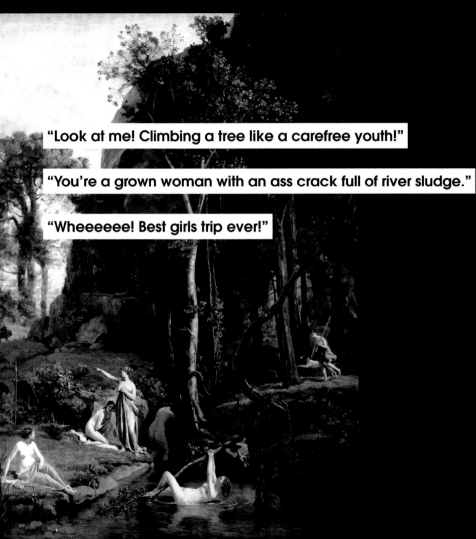

"Only the statues are supposed to be naked."

"Then they shouldn't call it a nude garden."

"They don't."

"You know what would make
this even better?"
"What?"
"Vodka."
"Check my bag.
I got you, girl."

"I promise to stay awake
past 10 p.m. this time."
"Maybe we should get
you some coke."
"Like soda?"
"Sure . . ."

"I just want to have an adventure like Thelma and Louise."

"I'm in, but can we cut out the driving-off-a-cliff thing?"

"But we're not wearing bathing suits."

"That didn't stop us at your grandma's birthday party."

"Okay, so the map was upside down this whole time."

"Oh my god."

"I don't know why you guys always give me the map."

"I think we did too many shrooms."

69

"You didn't say this was going to be a naked spa."

"It's not, but any spa is a naked spa if you have buns like ours."

"What should we do next? Prank call each other's crushes?"
"We're not twelve years old."
"You're right. Let's prank call each
other's crushes while drinking wine."

"Let's moon those people."

"Why doesn't anyone ever laugh at our hilarious stories?"

"Because we're obviously funnier than everybody else."

"Then we close the spell and recharge in the moon."

"Can we get to the margarita part?"

"You have to stop watching *Practical Magic*."

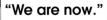

"Should this be our album cover?

Is it too late to play at Lilith Fair?"

"We're not in a band."

"We are now."

75

The
Super
Honest
Friend

"No, I don't think you need a boob job.
But I do think you should get them out of our tomatoes."

"We did it doggy style last night,
and I could not stop queefing."

"That's normal. Last time I did it
like that, my vagina sounded like
a one-woman brass band."

"If you were wearing the ugliest dress I've ever seen, like something a child sewed out of scraps from a dumpster, would you want me to tell you?"

"Sure, the men here all look like Scrooge McDuck, but it's been two years since you've been laid."

54

"I just think you can do better than someone who sleeps on an air mattress and rides his friend's sister's bicycle to work."

"The reason your date looks so sad is because your natural deodorant is not working.

I told you.

I've got some of the normal kind in my purse."

"I'm thinking about getting bangs."

"Remember when you got bangs in high school and everyone called you Lord Farquaad?"

"Good point."

"Do you think we're too close?"

"You mean because we share clothes and have the same hairstyle and poop with the door open so we can keep talking?"

"Yes."

"I keep telling you astrology isn't real. Stop choosing paint colors based on the alignment of the planets."

"Typical Virgo."

"This song is called 'You Are Buying Too Many Plants and This Is an Intervention.'"

89

"Reason #47 you're better off without Steve: he thought he didn't have to wash his butt because the shampoo dripped down there."

"Thank goodness she's cute. Heather's baby girl looked like Danny DeVito."

91

Art Credits

Pg	Title	Artist	Location
11	**Two Ladies**	Winslow Homer	The Metropolitan Museum of Art
12	**Two Ladies at their Sewing**	Alexander Hugo Bakker Korff	Rijksmuseum
13	**Young Wife: First Stew**	Lilly Martin Spencer	The Metropolitan Museum of Art
14	**Venus, Cupid and Ceres**	Cornelis Cornelisz van Haarlem	The Art Institute of Chicago
15	**Désirs**	William Sergeant Kendall	Smithsonian American Art Museum
16	**A Reading**	Thomas Wilmer Dewing	Smithsonian American Art Museum
18	**Portrait of the Three Regentesses of the Leprozenhuis, Amsterdam, Ferdinand Bol**	Anonymous	Rijksmuseum
19	**Two Women in Yellow Kerchiefs**	Constantin Guys	The Art Institute of Chicago
20	**Yellow Dancers (In the Wings)**	Edgar Degas	The Art Institute of Chicago
21	**Two Young Peasant Women**	Camille Pissarro	The Metropolitan Museum of Art
22	**Idle Hours**	Harry Siddons Mowbray	Smithsonian American Art Museum
24	**Girls and Flowers**	George Cochran Lambdin	Smithsonian American Art Museum
25	**Interior with Women beside a Linen Cupboard**	Pieter de Hooch	Rijksmuseum

26	**Spring**	Thomas Wilmer Dewing	Smithsonian American Art Museum
27	**Curiosity**	Gerard ter Borch the Younger	The Metropolitan Museum of Art
29	**The Favorite of the Emir**	Jean Joseph Benjamin Constant	The National Gallery of Art
30	**The Bathers**	William Adolphe Bouguereau	The Art Institute of Chicago
31	**Hermia and Helena**	Washington Allston	Smithsonian American Art Museum
32	**The Conversation**	Marcellin Gilbert Desboutin	The Art Institute of Chicago
33	**Woman in Bed, Profile, Getting Up**	Henri de Toulouse-Lautrec	The Art Institute of Chicago
34	**An Eclogue**	Kenyon Cox	Smithsonian American Art Museum
35	**Two Ladies Examining a Little Painting**	Alexander Hugo Bakker Korff	Rijksmuseum
36	**Self Portrait with Two Pupils**	Adelaide Labille-Guiard	The Metropolitan Museum of Art
37	**Scene From the Life of a Female Saint**	Antonio Vivarini	Detroit Institute of Arts
38	**Three Servant Women**	Constantin Guys	The Art Institute of Chicago
39	**Jupiter, in the Guise of Diana, and Callisto**	Francois Boucher	The Metropolitan Museum of Art
40	**Night and Her Daughter Sleep**	Mary L Macomber	Smithsonian American Art Museum
41	**The Fitting**	Mary Cassatt	The Metropolitan Museum of Art
42	**The Misses Mary and Hannah Murray**	John Trumbull	Smithsonian American Art Museum
43	**The Coleman Sisters**	Thomas Sully	The National Gallery of Art

45	The Muses Urania and Calliope	Simon Vouet	The National Gallery of Art
46	Two Women Reading in a Field	Arthur B. Davies	The Cleveland Museum of Art
47	Two Women at a Window	Bartolome Esteban Murillo	The National Gallery of Art
48	The Frankland Sisters	John Hoppner	The National Gallery of Art
49	Two Women in Day Dresses	Jules David	The Metropolitan Museum of Art
50	Luncheon with Figures in Masquerade Dress	Jean-Francois de Troy	Detroit Institute of Arts
51	The Appeal	Titian	Detroit Institute of Arts
52	Bathers Playing with a Crab	Pierre-Auguste Renoir	Cleveland Museum of Art
53	Standing and Reclining Nymphs	Louis M. Eilshemius	Smithsonian American Art Museum
54	At the Milliner's	Edgar Degas	The Metropolitan Museum of Art
55	Three Regentesses and the House Mother of the Amsterdam Lepers' Asylum	Werner van den Valckert	Rijksmuseum
56	Women in an Interior	Paul Delaroche	Cleveland Museum of Art
57	Two Washerwomen Crossing a Small Park in Paris	Jean Francois Raffaelli	The Art Institute of Chicago
58	Gossip	Giovanni Boldini	The Metropolitan Museum of Art
59	Two Women in Late Eighteenth Century Dress	William Edward Frost	The Art Institute of Chicago
61	Diana and Actaeon (Diana Surprised in Her Bath)	Camille Corot	The Metropolitan Museum of Art

62	**L'Automne**	Pierre Cecile Puvis De Chavannes	Smithsonian American Art Museum
63	**Before the Ballet**	Edgar Degas	The National Gallery of Art
64	**Mosquito Nets**	John Singer Sargent	Detroit Institute of Arts
65	**Madame Marsollier and Her Daughter**	Jean Marc Nattier	Detroit Institute of Arts
66	**Saint Margaret of Cortona**	Gaspare Traversi	The Metropolitan Museum of Art
67	**Figures on the Beach**	Auguste Renoir	The Metropolitan Museum of Art
68	**Italian Landscape with Three Women Making Music**	Gerard de Lairesse	Rijksmuseum
69	**The Perfume of Roses**	Charles C. Curran	Smithsonian American Art Museum
70	**Four Naked Women**	Albrecht Durer	Detroit Institute of Arts
71	**Water Lilies**	Walter Shirlaw	Smithsonian American Art Museum
72	**Girls at a Window**	Raimundo de Madrazo y Garreta	The Metropolitan Museum of Art
73	**Portrait of Charlotte and Sarah Carteret-Hardy**	Thomas Lawrence	Cleveland Museum of Art
74	**The Three Graces**	William Etty	The Metropolitan Museum of Art
75	**In the Garden**	Thomas Wilmer Dewing	Smithsonian American Art Museum
77	**Two Tahitian Women**	Paul Gauguin	The Metropolitan Museum of Art
78	**Mary Capel and Her Sister Elizabeth**	Sir Peter Lely	The Metropolitan Museum of Art

79	**A Friendly Call**	William Merritt Chase	The National Gallery of Art
80	**A Cherry Vendor at the Door**	Abraham van Strij (I)	Rijksmuseum
81	**In the Studio**	Alfred Stevens	The Metropolitan Museum of Art
82	**At the Moulin Rouge, La Goulue and Her Sister**	Henri de Toulouse-Lautrec	The Art Institute of Chicago
83	**Two Women in Classical Dress**	Claude Lorrain	The National Gallery of Art
84	**Majas on a Balcony**	Francisco de Goya y Lucientes	The Metropolitan Museum of Art
85	**Two Women in an Italian Landscape**	Miner Kilbourne Kellogg	Smithsonian American Art Museum
86	**Two Women**	Alfred H. Maurer	Smithsonian American Art Museum
87	**Two Women**	Ernst Ludwig Kirchner	Los Angeles County Museum of Art
88	**Music**	Thomas Wilmer Dewing	Smithsonian American Art Museum
89	**Lady Sarah Bunbury Sacrificing to the Graces**	Sir Joshua Reynolds	The Art Institute of Chicago
90	**Reading the Story of Oenone**	Francis Davis Millet	Detroit Institute of Arts
91	**Virgin and Child with Saint Catherine of Alexandria**	Anthony van Dyck	The Metropolitan Museum of Art